BRISTOL CITY BUSES

MIKE WALKER

AMBERLEY

This brief history of Bristol City Buses is dedicated to the thousands of employees, both male and female, who have kept the wheels of public transport in Bristol running for 138 years. Be they bus or tram drivers, conductors and inspectors, maintenance, clerical, supervisory or managerial staff, they have delivered a service to Bristol's travelling public through fair weather and foul and through conflict and peace. I am proud to have been counted among them.

Mike Walker
Wells
Somerset
January 2014

First published 2014

Amberley Publishing
The Hill, Stroud
Gloucestershire, GL5 4EP

www.amberley-books.com

Copyright © Mike Walker, 2014

The right of Mike Walker to be identified as the Author of this work has been asserted in accordance with the Copyrights, Designs and Patents Act 1988.

ISBN 978 1 4456 1775 6 (PRINT)
ISBN 978 1 4456 1793 0 (E-BOOK)

British Library Cataloguing in Publication Data.
A catalogue record for this book is available from the British Library.

Typeset in 9.5pt on 12pt Celeste.
Typesetting by Amberley Publishing.
Printed in the UK.

Introduction

Bristol City Buses is not intended to be a complete history. In fact, the buses that operated regularly on Bristol city bus services could only be truly identified during the Bristol Joint Services years between 1937 and 1978, and again after the Bristol Country services became a separate company in January 1986. However, by consultation of various documents, minutes and publications, the author has tried to give an overview of the development of the Bristol city buses and services from before the introduction of the first motor bus, when electric trams provided for the vast majority of public transport journeys, through a period of the monopoly operation of the services in the city by one operator, to the preparation for deregulation day, on 26 October 1986, when Bristol city bus services would, once again, experience free market competition.

Readers wishing to delve deeper into the subject are strongly recommended to read some of the publications listed in the Bibliography.

The Story

Bristol is a city built on maritime trade and by the middle of the nineteenth century the majority of employment in the city centred around the docks. The working classes lived close to their place of employment as a matter of necessity. During the Industrial Revolution Bristol expanded its manufacturing base and with it the population, and by the mid-1800s public transport as we would know it today arrived in the city in the shape of Brunel's Great Western Railway.

By 1870 the Corporation sought powers to establish a tramway in the city and the first line was laid from Perry Road (close to the central docks), west along Whiteladies Road to Apsley Road, although it did not get powers to operate the tram service, and so by 1875 a private company, the Bristol Tramways Company, was incorporated so as to operate the horse trams. By the turn of the century the city had a network of horse tram services and the company, having acquired the Bristol Cab Company, became the Bristol Tramways & Carriage Company Ltd (BT&CC), being renamed as the Bristol Omnibus Company Ltd in 1957.

From 1877 the company started a horse bus service as a feeder from the St George tram terminus to Kingswood. In the suburb of Clifton, particularly, the residents did not want a tram service to and from the city because of its association with the 'working class' and so a horse bus was introduced from there into the city in 1887.

The tram system was electrified by the turn of the century and the last line, to Westbury in the north-west, was laid down in 1908.

An article in the *Illustrated Bristol News* in 1962 declared that the Bristol Motor Company '...*opened up the first motor public transport system in the city...*' by 1900 '...*from the bottom of Blackboy Hill to the top of Westbury Hill...*' although no information was given as to when the service ceased. However, this operation preceded a 1905 BT&CC shareholders' meeting at which Sir George White stated that he had decided to replace the horse buses on the Westbury, Clifton and Ashton routes with motor buses so as to get working experience of their costs of operation. Sir George continued that a Thornycroft bus chassis had been delivered and was soon to be followed by eleven others, and the first motor bus service between the Victoria Rooms and Clifton Suspension Bridge started at 7.50 am on 17 January 1906, replacing the horse bus. Further services from outlying tram termini to areas outside of the city started soon afterwards.

The Thornycrofts were soon followed by buses manufactured by FIAT of Italy and Berliet of France. All proved unsuitable, the FIATs particularly so, with the result that BT&CC was successful in claiming damages from FIAT Motors of London for supplying vehicles that were unfit for the purpose for which they were intended. More importantly, however, the company decided that they could do a better job of building buses themselves, leading to the establishment of the Motor Constructional Works of the company, which became Bristol Commercial Vehicles and a world leader in innovative bus and coach design and production until it finally closed its doors in 1983.

Now that the BT&CC had decided to progress motor bus operation, and indeed motor bus construction, the motor bus was to reign supreme. Before the outbreak of hostilities in 1914 the company had added some 120 motor buses to its fleet, the majority of which had been constructed by the company themselves, although not all were for operation in the city.

Like many towns and cities during the Great War, Bristol lost many of its citizens to the armed forces as well as a number of its vehicles to the War Department. By January 1917 women were taken on as conductors (or 'clippies') for the trams, and the 1917 city timetable issued by the company showed six motor bus services in addition to the then fifteen tramways services, although most of these motor bus routes were suspended during hostilities.

By the beginning of 1919 further motor bus routes had been added, but again the timetable produced at the time declared that: '*It is the intention of the company to resume the services of the buses that have been withdrawn as soon as circumstances allow. The commandeering of buses by the War Department, and the shortage of men, through them joining the Colours, necessitates the withdrawal of the services.*'

Production of Bristol bus chassis (and bodies) to the pre-war design resumed in 1920, and by 1921 a further 168 buses of their own manufacture had been added to the fleet. Many of these were of a new type, the 4-tonner, which was a normal control high frame single-decker.

By 1921 BT&CC encountered some competition from a new company which had been set up as a charabanc operator in 1919. Greyhound Motors, as it was called, introduced one city service that year, with a further four routes in the following year. However, as a result of complaints from members of the public, the city council Watch Committee sought to regulate the expansion of motor bus operation, especially with a view to reducing competition with the established tramway network.

Another operator, Charles Russett, also started motor bus operations, and a report from the December 1922 Watch Committee meeting stated that: *'Licences for the following three months would be: Bristol Tramways, 47 city, 39 country and 9 spares, Greyhound Motors, 12 city with 3 spares and Charles Russett 3 city, 1 country and 1 spare.'* Thereafter new routes continued to be introduced across the radial tramway network, linking city suburbs, and Greyhound was at the forefront of innovation when it introduced a new style of double deck motor bus to the city, operating on their route between the Tramways Centre and Fishponds (route 'C'). Some of the Tramway company's first motor buses were double-deckers, but the first few weeks of operational experience had resulted in their conversion to single-deckers: the new Greyhound buses were of a different design altogether, being AEC NS-type buses with a cranked, lower, frame, and identical to those operating for London General in the capital.

During the middle of 1926 a new road was opened along the Avon Gorge from Hotwells westwards to Avonmouth. Initially it was suggested that a fast tramway would provide the public transport links, but in the event a new motor bus service was introduced linking Avonmouth and the Hotwells tramway terminal, shared between BT&CC and Greyhound.

On 31 March 1928 the Tramway Company acquired Greyhound Motors and with it eight city bus routes, although it would continue to be operated as a subsidiary company with its own identity for a number of years thereafter. In the same year the Tramway's Motor Constructional Works introduced its most successful bus chassis to date, the single deck B type, and the company quickly introduced this advanced bus on city services.

With Greyhound now in the control of BT&CC, and the acquisition of Russett in 1929, a monopoly existed in the provision of bus and tram services in the city, and this was consolidated by the 1930 Road Traffic Act which introduced national regulations and controls on the operation of motor bus and coach services.

Also in 1929 control of the company passed to the Great Western Railway (GWR). However, as the GWR did not have the necessary powers to operate street tramways, by 1930 they had passed control to their subsidiary company, the Western National Omnibus Company. During that year the company became part of the national Tilling group, this organization now becoming responsible for the trams and buses in the city.

The Motor Constructional Works produced their first modern double deck bus chassis in 1931, the petrol engined G-type, and despite not initially operating them in their own fleet they sent a number of demonstrators to other operators in the hope of getting orders. When the buses returned to Bristol they were allocated to the Greyhound fleet. By the mid-1930s Bristol model types had reached the J single deck chassis and the company took into stock a number of these for operation in the city.

In 1935 the company took new G-type double-deckers into its own fleet, and in January 1936 the Greyhound fleet was fully absorbed into the Tramway company with the remaining grey and white buses being repainted into the Bristol blue and white. In addition, during the same year, the local operator Bence of Hanham was also fully absorbed, having been taken over initially in 1930. The Bence services did not penetrate the city but connected many of the eastern suburbs (most of which were outside of the city and county boundary) with the trams at Staple Hill, Kingswood and Hanham.

The 1870 Tramways Act had given the city a recurring 7-year option to purchase the tramway system and in 1936 the city sought to exercise this right. Consequently the Bristol Transport Act 1937 allowed for both parties to take an equal share in a new body, to be known as Bristol Joint Services (hereinafter referred to as BJS). The new organization would be managed by an equal number of members from each side, to be known as 'A' (city) and 'B' (company) members, the nomenclature of which would identify the problems related to the joint operation until the end of BJS some 40 years later. When tramway replacement bus services were eventually introduced and extended beyond the existing city boundary to new housing estates, the mileage operated beyond the agreed boundaries was referred to as 'B' (or company) mileage, and when operated by BJS buses and crews, records had to be kept to ensure that either balancing mileage was operated by pure company vehicles on 'A' sections of the route, or a cash payment made to 'balance the books'.

The formation of BJS also allowed for the first definitive indication of the size of the city bus fleet: in order to identify the BJS buses for accounting purposes a 'C' prefix was added to their fleet number. On formation, 134 single deck buses were allocated this prefix, these being mostly of the Bristol B-type, together with fifty-four G-type double-deckers, and, of course, the electric tramcars. A further double-decker, the first of a new design, the K-type, intended to be powered only by an oil engine, was delivered in the middle of the year. At the inaugural BJS board meeting the chairman, and Tilling group managing director, Mr Heaton, in discussing orders for tram replacement motor buses, stated that, in his opinion, '... *"Bristol" vehicles were equal to any on the market'*. He also drew attention to the benefits of standardising the fleet, as well as allowing for the employment of local labour. At the time of the meeting, in addition to the trams, there were twenty-four motor bus routes, numbered between 18 and 282! Also discussed was the garaging of the post tram replacement motor buses, since the company felt that a number of tram depots would not be suitable for the new methods of operation. The following allocation of the required 417 city motor buses was proposed:

Avonmouth	8 buses
Brislington	61 buses
Eastville	64 buses
Lawrence Hill	111 buses
Muller Road	75 buses
Winterstoke Road	98 buses

The sites at Muller Road and Winterstoke Road were proposed as new motor bus depots to replace tram facilities at Horfield, Staple Hill, St George and Bedminster, while it was felt that the tram sheds at Brislington and Eastville could be converted for motor bus use.

The new K type chassis with double deck bodies by the company's own body works or Eastern Coach Works at Lowestoft (another Tilling group subsidiary) were delivered in large numbers for tram replacement during 1938 and 1939 and by the end of 1939 181 of these had arrived. The tram abandonment programme, however, did not go to plan, and was delayed again and again due to the start of hostilities in 1939, although by the outbreak of war a number of routes had in fact been abandoned and replaced by the brand new blue and white double deck 'K'-types. Further buses that had been ordered for tram replacement continued to be delivered and were stored at depots until required.

The new Winterstoke Road depot had been built and occupied just before the outbreak of war, and construction had started on the new Muller Road depot, but in the event both of these premises were requisitioned by the Air Ministry for war work and were replaced with Bellman hangers supplied by them and located near to the depot sites.

In 1940 an air raid damaged the Bedminster tram shed and forced the replacement of the Ashton Gate and Bedminster trams by buses, and the abandonment of the remaining parts of the system was again delayed until the spring of 1941, although in the event, on 11 April 1941 a stray bomb landed on the bridge over the river next to the Tramway's power station in central Bristol and severed the main cable supplying power to the remaining tramway network, which was instantly put out of action. Some buses immediately replaced tram services, and by the end of the month all of the stored buses had been put into service and the tramway was no more.

New K-type double-deckers continued to be delivered in 1940 and 1941, along with ten of the single deck equivalent, the L-type, but Bristol bus production soon ceased so that the factory could concentrate on war work, and the following year BJS received the first of a batch of twenty-seven petrol-engined Bedford single-deckers that it had been allocated by the Ministry of Supply. The city's buses gradually lost their blue and white livery to be replaced with olive, khaki or matt grey, and because of the large increase in the number of employees required at the aircraft factories and the docks, a number of additional buses were borrowed from other operators. Bus driving during the Second World War remained a reserved occupation, although because of the numbers of staff joining the forces and the increase in factory working, labour was in short supply, and so the company appointed over 100 auxiliary conductors, who often had other jobs but regularly worked part time so as to control boarding and alighting and help the regular conductor in working an often very full bus.

Because of both the docks and the number of factories devoted to war work the city was under constant attention from enemy bombers. On 28 August 1942 the city, and the Joint Services, were severely affected when a single bomb landed in Broad Weir, near Old Market, and destroyed three double-deck buses, killing almost fifty passengers as well as seriously injuring almost half that number. Among the casualties were seven members of the company's staff.

As the threat of invasion retreated the city's buses emerged from their drab wartime garb into the one of the Tilling organisation's two new corporate colour scheme, green and cream (the other being red and cream), the first examples being seen in service in 1944. Subsequent new buses would carry this livery, the Bristol blue having gone forever. By the end of the war in 1945 the company faced the major task of returning the service to normality, updating the fleet and repairing and replacing war damage. For a number of years following cessation of hostilities new buses would be hard to obtain. While continuing to maintain that buses of Bristol manufacture were the preferred option, at a BJS board meeting in 1946 the BJS and Tilling group chairman declared that, in order to overcome the shortage of new 'Bristol' buses, the Tilling organization had placed an order for 150 Leyland Titan double-deck buses and that fifty of these could be allocated to the BJS fleet. These Leyland buses would assist the Board in its declared intention that, where possible, the city services should be operated by a majority double-deck fleet, so as to both increase capacity and if necessary reduce some service frequencies to counter the staff shortage. It was agreed however that there would still be a limited requirement for single-deck vehicles.

The Transport Act 1947 was introduced by the Labour Government who were elected after the war with a mandate for, among other things, the nationalisation of transport industries, and during September 1948 it was announced that the Tilling organisation, and along with it BT&CC, would be so nationalised.

Deliveries of K-type double-deckers and L-type single-deckers continued throughout the late 1940s, together with the fifty Leyland Titans, and a major programme was put into place to refurbish the pre-war and just post-war vehicles that were suffering from heavy use, with a comprehensive plan to establish the diesel engine as the preferred means of propulsion. To this end, just before the war, the Motor Constructional Works developed a new engine, termed the AVW, which eventually became the standard power unit for the city's bus fleet. In 1949 a new prototype double-decker emerged from the Motor Constructional Works in the shape of the first Lodekka, a radical design which enabled the lower deck central gangway to be dropped and a lower overall build achieved: the new bus, registered LHY949, received the fleet number C5000, and after a demonstration tour to other Tilling companies, settled down to a normal working life in the city.

The development of the Lodekka, however, was a slow process: BJS continued to take delivery of the K-type, and, when the legally allowed dimensions of buses and coaches changed in 1950, the revised KS (7 ft 6 in wide) and KSW (8 ft wide) became the new standards, with four-bay sixty seat bodywork and open platforms. The L-type was also adapted to meet the new dimensions, but BJS ceased taking the model in 1950, when it received its last batch of thirty-three-seat dual doorway L5G and L6B models. These were to be the last new single-deck buses for the city for eleven years.

Even though the Lodekka had entered production in 1953, a 1954 BJS meeting decided that, although a small batch of these low buses would be useful for services to new housing estates where they would be required to operate under low bridges, the KSW would remain the standard BJS bus and this small batch of Lodekka buses were taken into stock in 1955. By 1957, when the production of the KSW ceased, 247 had been put into service, representing over half of the city's bus fleet at that time. Also in 1955 the Motor Constructional Works had been formed into a separate company, Bristol Commercial Vehicles Limited, and although close links would continue to be maintained between BT&CC and the new company, BT&CC would no longer manufacture its own bus chassis.

The development of the city route network continued throughout the 1950s as the city established new housing estates. Some of this development was taking place on land that had been added to the city from neighbouring Somerset in 1951, and was the subject of some discussion at board meetings as the company insisted that this territory had previously been part of their operation and therefore any routes crossing the existing city boundary into the new estates should be B' mileage, and therefore the revenue benefits from the newly built estates would favour the company rather than the Joint Services.

In 1956 the BJS Board agreed the purchase of 550 Setright ticket machines for city operations to replace the traditional Bell Punch machines with their rack of separate tickets that had been in use since the early tram operations. The new machines were to make ticket issuing quicker and easier and simplify accounting and cash reconciliation.

The biggest shake up of the city service network since the tram abandonment took place in September 1958 when a new country bus and coach station was opened at Marlborough Street, on the site of the old Whitson Street tram permanent way depot. For the first time the departure point of the country services from Bristol, and the garaging of the vehicles that operated them, came under one roof, and with it came the opportunity to relocate the central stopping points for many of the city bus routes.

1960 saw the entry into service of what was in time to become the new standard bus for city services: development of the Lodekka had progressed to the production of a completely flat floor model and a further revision to the maximum permitted dimensions allowed for a 30 feet long double-deck bus. The first of this type was produced in 1959, finished as Joint Services LC8540, 995EHW, and was a front entrance seventy-seat model termed the FLF (*Front entrance, Long, Flat floor*). Like its predecessor, C5000, the new bus spent some time being demonstrated to other Tilling group companies, and eventually entered service in the city along with eleven similar vehicles in 1960.

In 1961 the city services received five underfloor-engined forty-five-seat Bristol MW saloons to replace a number of the half cab Bristol L buses, although by this time many of the city's original two doorway thirty-three-seat L types had been exchanged with the country services for similar thirty-five-seat rear entrance models, so that the company could use the front door on these two doorway models to enable the bus to be one man operated.

In 1963 the BJS operation came under national scrutiny as it was revealed that the company in Bristol operated a colour bar, and that although immigrants were employed by the company outside of Bristol, and on the maintenance staff, some years earlier the Trades Unions had passed a resolution that their members would not work with Commonwealth staff in the city. The ethnic community in the city organised a bus boycott, supported by others in the city, especially students, and demonstrations took place at the May Day Rally in Bristol, when up to 200 men and women (mostly black working people) took part in what may have been the first black-led march against racial discrimination in the country. The world famous cricketer Sir Learie Constantine, who was in Bristol for a match between Gloucestershire and the West Indies, became involved in his capacity as High Commissioner for Trinidad and Tobago, and after getting no satisfaction with meetings in the city, took the matter to the Transport Holding Company (which had replaced the British Transport Commission). Eventually, on 28 August 1963, it was reported that the colour bar on Bristol's buses had ended and that ethnic crews would now be able to join the platform staff.

As a direct result of the appointment of a new General Manager, Mr J. T. E. Robinson, a new fleet name style appeared in 1965, with a gold Bristol scroll, of the type that had been synonymous with Bristol-built bus and lorry chassis, and indeed Bristol aeroplanes. This replaced the block capital BRISTOL on the side panels, which itself had replaced the city arms on the sides of buses in 1961. However, it was later agreed that a smaller version of the city arms would be carried on BJS bus side panels above the new scroll fleetname.

In September 1966 a new *City Centre Circle* service was introduced, linking the central shopping area and Temple Meads Railway Station with the coach and car parking facilities that had been established at the edge of the now declining central docks at Canons Marsh. Although by this time the BJS fleet had a small number of the MW underfloor-engined forty-five-seat single-deckers, these remained two-man operated and so this new service was operated by company owned MW and LS buses that were based at Lawrence Hill depot and were modified to operate one-man country services from the Bristol Bus Station. This service was unique in using specially purchased Almex ticket machines which produced a one fare ticket.

By 1966 the BJS service network had been revised and renumbered, as part of a company-wide route numbering scheme, so that city service route numbers ran from 1 to 99, although, as part of the route numbering system some suffix letters were retained. It was explained in contemporary timetable booklets that the suffix letter C indicated a normally cross city route that was to terminate at the central area, L indicated a journey of a local nature, such as a peak hour short working or duplicate or, perhaps, a journey finishing at a depot, with F, H and J indicating factory extensions and K a school bus.

The first conversion of an existing BJS service to one-man operation took place in 1968. In a previous service revision route 19 had been formed by combining the two separate city routes, where low bridges required the use of single-deck buses, into one route. Now the conductors were removed and the buses were converted so that the driver could take the fares as passengers boarded. Like many bus operators, BJS had experienced their largest passenger growth in the 1950s and by the end of that decade passenger numbers began to decline, principally because of the growth of the private motor car. Car use also caused traffic congestion, which adversely affected the running of the services, and this, coupled with the difficulty in employing and retaining staff in a time of high employment, increased the costs of operation while reducing patronage and with it the revenue earned.

Following the successful conversion of service 19 to one-man operation it was decided that further conversions of this type should take place in an effort to reduce operating costs and improve service reliability, as only one member of staff would henceforth be required to operate each journey.

It was expected that BJS would take the FLF Lodekka's replacement, the newly designed Bristol VR *(VR indicated that the engine was placed Vertically at the Rear)*, and it was declared in an article in the *Bristol Evening Post* in 1966 that twenty-eight of this new type of double-deck bus would soon enter service on city routes, and that they would be operated without a conductor at off-peak times. In the event, however, the order was cancelled and replaced by one for single-deck buses suitable for one-man operation.

These new single-deckers were to be of the recently introduced Bristol RE (*Rear Engined*) model, built to a new length of 36 feet, and after discussions with the city staff representatives the order for these new buses was amended so that they were fitted with a second, central, doorway in order to speed up passenger flow when the buses were operated without a conductor. This delayed their delivery, and so when the next two services in the city were converted to operate without a conductor in January 1969, single-door country service RE saloons were used until the dual-doorway buses were delivered later in that year.

The delivery of new single-deckers and the conversion of city services to one-man operation continued apace and by 1973 155 dual doorway RE saloons were in use in the BJS fleet. As a result of a productivity agreement reached with the traffic staff representatives in the early 1970s many busy two-man operated routes had their conductors removed during the evenings and on Sundays, reducing the unreliability caused by staff shortages and increasing the earning potential of driving staff which, in turn, aided staff recruitment.

In 1972 BJS put into service its first one-man operated double-deck buses, being a small batch of eight two-doorway Bristol VRTs which were used to part convert service 22/23 to one-man operation, alongside two-doorway single-deckers.

The VRT *(VRT described the engine position - Vertical Rear Transverse)* became the new standard double-deck bus for city operation, with 112 intended for BJS before the last of the type arrived in 1980, although single-deckers were delivered alongside the new double-deckers. The 'RE' was replaced by the new National Bus Company standard 'Leyland National', around fifty being delivered new or acquired second-hand later in their life.

The National Bus Company had taken over from the Transport Holding Company on 1 January 1969, becoming the owner of Bristol Omnibus Company, and was therefore the new partner in the BJS agreement. The National Bus Company had a mandate to 'break even, taking one year with another', which put pressure on the working relationship within BJS since the city council, representing the concerns of their ratepayers, disagreed strongly with the continuing cycle of fare rises and service reductions. In addition, as a result of the 1972 Local Government Act, a new local authority in the form of Avon County Council became involved as they had been given a statutory duty to be responsible for public transport services. Avon County Council refused to recognize the city as a bus operator under the 1937 Bristol Transport Act, leaving the city council reluctant to support proposed fare increase until this matter was resolved.

Discussions around this disagreement continued, especially about how to deal with falling passenger numbers, increased costs and traffic congestion, and yet balance the books. Finally, after a directive from the Regional Director of National Bus Company that BJS had to be made financially self-supporting, agreement was reached that the BJS partnership would be dissolved on 15 August 1978, ending four decades of involvement of the city council in the operation of the city's bus services. In general terms the agreement resulted in the company retaining the buses while the city gained the depots (except Lawrence Hill, which operated mixed services and was the home of the central repair works), and these were leased back to the company.

After dissolution of the agreement the company moved quickly to reorganize the city services so as to serve many of the dormitory estates and towns that had been built at the edge of the city and which previously had been served by country buses, and the C prefix and special fleet name that identified the former BJS buses were quickly removed. The company was now free to integrate the former BJS vehicles into the rest of the fleet and to do with them what it wanted.

In common with other National Bus Company subsidiaries, the Bristol company had undertaken the *Market Analysis Project* with a view to aligning the service provided with demand. The resultant service revisions were introduced in October 1981, and apart from rationalising the services, a network of limited stop routes was offered, operating from a number of out of town estates into the city at regular intervals, eventually to be branded as *City Clipper*.

In a continuing process of reducing costs, the removal of conductors from city services continued apace, and as the former BJS FLF double-deckers became time expired, or beyond economic repair, they were often replaced in the city by similar vehicles of this type released from the country services.

In 1981 the Secretary of State for Transport referred the company's operation of Bristol city services to the Monopolies and Mergers Commission, to determine if it were abusing its monopoly position in the city. The findings concluded that, because of the National Bus Company's *Market Analysis Project*, the operating efficiency of the city services had improved from 74.1 per cent to 88.9 per cent, achieved by a rationalisation of the route network and a tightening up of the vehicle and crew schedules, and although this had resulted in a further reduction in the fleet size (of around 20 per cent), it had provided savings and increased efficiencies that would be of benefit to the people of Bristol.

New double-deck bus deliveries for the city operation resumed in 1982 with the new

Leyland model, the Bristol-built Olympian, and these together with subsequent new buses were delivered with just a single door: although there were protracted negotiations with the staff representatives, these were eventually accepted for single manning on city services.

Apart from buying a small number of second-hand VRs in 1982, further Olympians were taken into stock in 1983, the last of which ended the company's 75-year history of operating buses built in the city, as the chassis production plant closed in that year. In the summer of that year the National Bus Company announced that Bristol Omnibus Company would be split into smaller and more locally responsive units, and this would eventually (by 1 January 1986) leave Bristol Omnibus Company *only* operating city services. The country services, although operating in and out of the city, would henceforth be provided by a new company, to be called *Badgerline*.

The 1984 White Paper *Buses* proposed that the 50-year-old system of bus route licencing should be abolished and replaced by the deregulation of local bus operation in which the operator could register those routes that they wanted to run commercially while any socially necessary services which were not so registered were to be put out to tender by the local authority. In addition, the National Bus Company, of which the Bristol company was a subsidiary, was to be broken up and sold into the private sector. It was also in 1984, in July, that the last conventional forward-engined bus in regular service, the FLF Lodekka, was withdrawn from the streets of Bristol. Bus conductors were no longer to feature on regular bus services in the city and the network was now one-man operated.

Unsure of the future of the company due to the impending privatisation and deregulation, the management team sought to consolidate their position by preparing the commercial network that they would implement at the advent of deregulation in October 1986. The company took no new buses in 1985, although on 29 April of that year, it announced a new identity with a new livery of red, blue and yellow. In 1986 the company received 170 new minibuses of Ford and Mercedes manufacture, all painted in the bright new livery and marketed as *City Dart*, since more frequent, shorter, routes were to be implemented so as to defend the company's operation against any possible competition, and in fact a number of these service alterations and enhancements were introduced in the period leading up to October.

26 October 1986 was deregulation day, and for the first time since the 1930 Road Traffic Act the bus services in Bristol city were now open to free competition.

It is believed that the first horse buses operated by the Bristol Tramways company in the city were new in 1877 for a tram feeder service to and from St George. The Clifton service was the first regular horse bus route that served the city, operated here by four-bay bus number 83. (*BMG&AP9412*)

It is recorded that the three-bay horse buses were newer than the four-bay ones. Number 31 is shown operating from the Drawbridge (which became the Tramways Centre) to Clifton (the 'High Level Station' of the Clifton Rocks Railway), adjacent to the Clifton Suspension Bridge. (*M. J. Tozer Collection*)

Another three-bay bus in the company of horse trams at what was by then the Tramways Centre: a pair of trace horses passes in the opposite direction. (*Allen Janes collection*)

Trace horses have been attached to three bay bus 29 for the climb up Park Street. (*G. D. Hodgson*)

A view up Park Street, showing the steepness of the climb and the reason for the attaching of an extra pair of horses on the Clifton route. At the top of the hill a horse tram can be seen crossing the top of Park Street on the original horse tram route. (*BMG&AP9356*)

A three-bay Clifton horse bus marked for the Suspension Bridge is shown at the Tramways Centre. (*Peter Davey Collection*)

An early four-bay horse bus - which looks like number 105 - on the tramway feeder route to Ashley Down. (*BVBG*)

An early four-bay horse bus on Durdham Down operating the service linking Westbury with the Redland tram terminus, withdrawn when the tramway was extended to Westbury. (*BMG&AP5130*)

An earlier four-bay horse bus at the 1842-built Victoria Rooms operating to and from Clifton Suspension Bridge. (*M. J. Tozer Collection*)

17

By 1900 this Daimler 'Wagonette' is believed to have operated Bristol's first motor bus service from Blackboy Hill, adjacent to Durdham Down, to Westbury Hill. Registration numbers were not introduced until 1904. (*BMG&AP14376*)

AE726 was numerically the Tramway company's second Thornycroft, put into service on 17 January 1906 between the Victoria Rooms and Brunel's Clifton Suspension Bridge. The bodywork was by the United Electric Car Company in Preston. (*Allen Janes Collection*)

The rear view of the open rear platform of the first Thornycroft, AE725, at Merchants Road, Clifton, on its first day in service. (*Allen Janes Collection*)

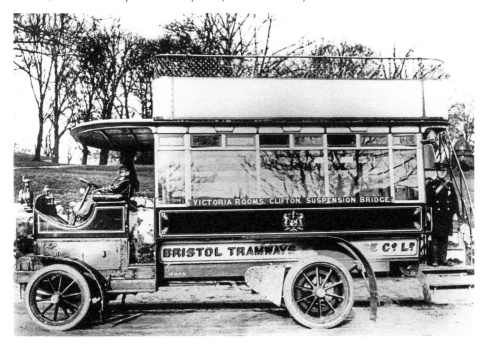

A Berliet chassis from 1909 fitted with double-deck bodywork by the United Electric Car Company operating on the original motor bus route. The three Berliet buses lasted barely three years. (*M. J. Tozer Collection*)

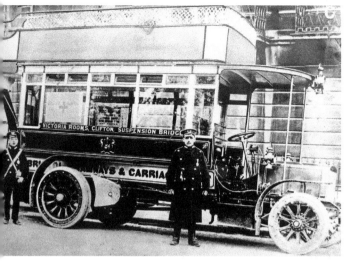

A Thornycroft bus shown here operating the Victoria Rooms to Clifton route. There were twelve of these used to inaugurate the Bristol Tramway company's motor bus services. (*Peter Davey Collection*)

Having lost its upper deck seating, this Thornycroft is shown operating a tramway feeder service from Brislington through Keynsham to Saltford, outside of the Bristol city operating area. The Tramway company at one time envisaged operating trams along this route so as to connect with the Bath trams at Saltford. (*BMG&AP9416*)

Thornycroft AE725 again, but this time with a new Bristol-built 'all season' body. The bus is operating a tram feeder service from Filton, north Bristol, towards Patchway and beyond. Patchway was eventually served by city buses. (*BMG&AP9585*)

AE736 was also a Thornycroft, re-bodied with a Bristol-built body in 1910 and surviving until 1914. (*BMG&AP9471*)

AE772 is one of the first Bristol-built vehicles, a C40 type constructed in 1908 with Bristol's own bodywork. It is believed to have lasted until 1923. (*BVBG*)

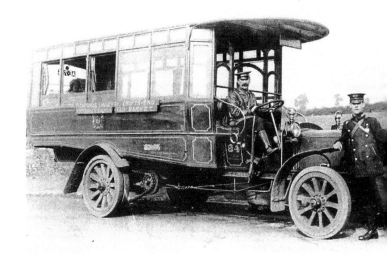

A Thornycroft chassis rebuilt with Bristol's own bodywork operating between Old Market and Fishponds. (*Allen Janes Collection*)

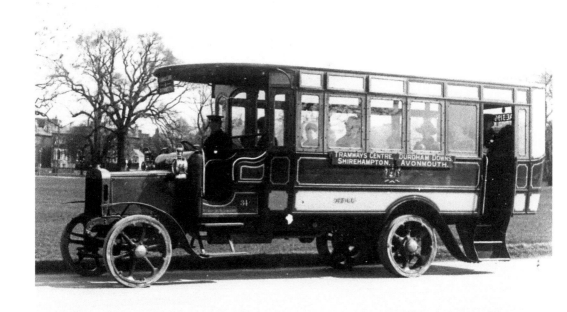

AE3196 was a 1914 Bristol C60 with Bristol's own 28-seat bodywork operating the long 28 service between the Tramways Centre and Avonmouth to the north-west of the city, introduced in 1908. (*BVBG*)

AE2785, a Bristol-bodied Bristol C45 of 1913, stands outside the Tramway Company's Clifton Rocks Railway, which connected Clifton with Hotwells below. (*M. J. Tozer Collection*)

The last Bristol C45 to be built in 1913, AE2782, again fitted with Bristol's own bodywork. (*BVBG*)

AE3163 was a 1912 Bristol C45 with the company's own 22-seat body. By the time that this photograph was taken the original motor bus route to Clifton had been extended back to the Tramways Centre. (*M. J. Tozer Collection*)

1914-built Bristol C50 AE3781, with a 1917-built 24-seat body, was one of several buses fitted with a gas bag on the roof so as to enable it to operate on town gas during the 1914–1918 war. (*BVBG*)

One vehicle was new to the company in 1915, Bristol 'W' type AE4973, the prototype for what was to become the Bristol 4-tonner. It entered service on the Clifton route, service 18, in March of that year. (*Peter Davey Collection*)

Bristol bus production was put on hold between 1915 and 1919 because of the Great War, and resumed with the 4-ton model. HT2112 was a 1920-built bus with a second hand Bristol-built 28-seat dual-door body. (*BVBG*)

1921-built 4-ton model HT2649 with Bristol's 29-seat rear-entrance bodywork shown operating to Clifton on the 18 service. (*Peter Davey Collection*)

As bus designs improved they became more complicated, but the underside of this 4-ton model shows that they were still simple in the 1920s! (*Peter Davey Collection*)

HT5336, a 1922 Bristol 4-ton model with Bristol's 30-seat dual-doorway bodywork, outside the Victoria Rooms operating service 20 between Sneyd Park, the Centre and Bedminster. (*BVBG*)

Bristol 4-ton models at Colston Avenue on the Centre. The front bus, HT5745, dates from 1922 and is operating service 21 to Ashley Down Road, north Bristol, while the bus behind is operating country service 26 to Frampton Cotterell via Winterbourne. (*Peter Davey Collection*)

Although Bristol built the A-type as a single or double-deck chassis, the operating company took only one of them, 32-seat single deck HU4325. It is shown here operating in the city between Eastville and Durdham Down. (*Peter Davey Collection*)

A pneumatic-tyred dual-door Bristol 4-ton bus at speed on the Portway, the new link road to Avonmouth built alongside the River Avon in 1926. (*Peter Davey Collection*)

A Bristol 4-ton model at Prince Street, the central area terminus of the 99 service to Avonmouth when, between 1928 and 1930, it was extended back from Hotwells. (*Peter Davey Collection*)

Believed to have been taken around 1925, dual-door Bristol 4-ton HT5737 from 1922 is operating city service 83. (*'Omnibus', Bristol Omnibus staff magazine*)

Alongside the 4-ton model, Bristol built this small 2-ton bus, and although it was built in 1925 it was fitted with solid tyres. Route number 95, shown in the back window, was a Westbury-on-Trym, Henbury, Brentry circular service, these areas eventually being served by BJS routes. (*BVBG*)

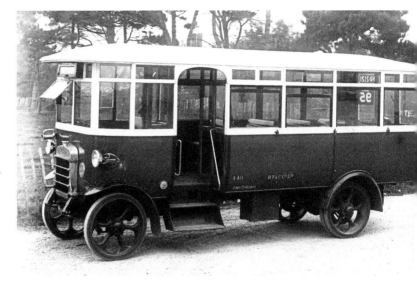

The competing Pioneer fleet of Charles Russett was taken over by the Tramway company in 1929. HT4358, one of their buses operating in the city, between Old Market and Fishponds, was a 1921 3-ton Dennis with a 30-seat Morrish front-entrance body. (*Geoff Bruce Collection*)

Greyhound Motors favoured Dennis vehicles, HT5322 being a 4-ton model with Strachan & Brown 32-seat body, operating their route C from the Centre to Fishponds. (*M. J. Tozer Collection*)

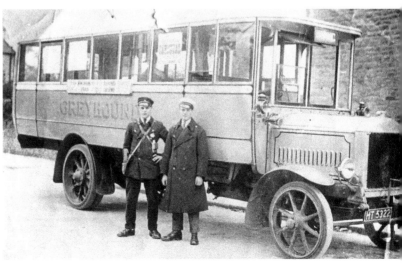

Greyhound Motors HU991 was also a 4-ton Dennis with a similar body, apparently with sliding roof panels. The Sneyd Park–Centre–Railway Station–Bedminster Down route was their service A. (*BVBG*)

Greyhound Motors' first double-deck buses arrived in 1926. HU3524 was one of three AEC 409 models, with 52-seat outside staircase bodywork by Short Brothers. These, and subsequent buses, were later fitted with roofs and pneumatic tyres. The bus is on route C between the Centre and Fishponds. (*BMG&AP9468*)

Operating on the Tramway company's route to Fishponds, service 84, is HU4811, the first of the 1926 delivery of Bristol 4-ton buses. (*BVBG*)

AEC 409 model of Greyhound Motors, HU3526, after being fitted with a roof, but still with solid tyres. (*M. J. Tozer Collection*)

C372, HW8363, was a Bristol B-type built in 1930 with Bristol's own 31-seat dual doorway body and is seen on the Centre operating to Temple Meads Railway Station on service 18 with the company's mock Tudor office behind. (*Peter Davey Collection*)

HY6198 was an early Bristol G-type, built in 1932 with a Beadle 52-seat body, and allocated to the subsidiary Greyhound Motors fleet, becoming C3002 with the 1937 fleet renumbering and the formation of BJS. It is shown undergoing a tilt test, presumably before entering service. (*M. J. Tozer Collection*)

An offside view of HY6198 while in service with Greyhound Motors operating the 84 route to Downend, east Bristol. (*BVBG*)

The three Bristol Tramways G-types built in 1932 were used initially as demonstrators. This is G116, HY6896, with a Beadle 52-seat body, which entered service in Bristol in September 1933, becoming C3004 in 1937. (*Peter Davey Collection*)

AAE250 was a 1933-built Bristol B-type with Bristol's own 30-seat dual doorway body. This bus became C540 in 1937, and is seen at the Cheltenham Road Arches on service 89 to the Clifton Suspension Bridge. (*M. J. Tozer Collection*)

Two 1936 Bristol G-types are seen at the Redland terminus of service 20, the far bus being CHY120 which is loading for Bedminster, the closest being DAE374, showing a destination for the Tramways Centre, and both with Bristol's own bodywork. They became C3043 and C3053 respectively. (*S. Miles Davey*)

C3115, EHY577, a 1938 Bristol-bodied 56-seat Bristol K5G, was placed in service in May of that year to replace part of the tram network and is shown on Durdham Down operating tram replacement route 1 between the Centre and Westbury. (*Peter Davey Collection*)

A view inside of Lawrence Hill depot before the start of hostilities. From left to right the vehicles are: B-types 322, HW3109, dating from 1928 and AAE178, new in 1935 and renumbered as C538; and DHY657, 2205, a 1937 32-seat Duple-bodied Bristol JO6A coach. (*Peter Davey Collection*)

CHW51 was one of a batch of thirteen J-types new in 1936, eventually becoming C2701 when fitted with a Gardner diesel engine. It suffered body damage during the war but was rebuilt and returned to service. Service 142 operated between Temple Meads and Filton via Henleaze and Southmead. (*Peter Davey Collection*)

In late 1938 the company borrowed JML784 from AEC Ltd. It was a Regent O661 with a Weymann 56-seat body, and operated for BJS for a few months before being returned. It is seen here at the Durdham Down terminus of tram replacement route 2 between here, Old Market and Stapleton. (*S. Miles Davey*)

The motor bus takes over! A brand new K-type operating along Whiteladies Road from The Centre to Westbury-on-Trym on Monday 9 May 1938, the trams to Westbury having ended on 7 May. (*S. Miles Davey*)

Wartime conditions demanded the white painted wings and masked headlights, as shown by C432, HY1965, new in 1931 as B682. The bus is standing at the Tramways Centre bound for Sea Mills to the west of the city. (*George Vowles*)

C3257, FHT830, was part of a batch of Bristol K5Gs delivered for the replacement of the trams to Filton and the Downs in July 1939, and is seen here in Sea Mills Square in wartime conditions. (*George Vowles*)

Bristol B-type HW6636 started life in 1929 as a London Lorries-bodied 26-seat coach. During the war years it was re-bodied by Bence of Hanham with a 28-seat bus body with perimeter seating so as to allow more standing room. The Bence bus operating business had been acquired in 1930. (*George Vowles*)

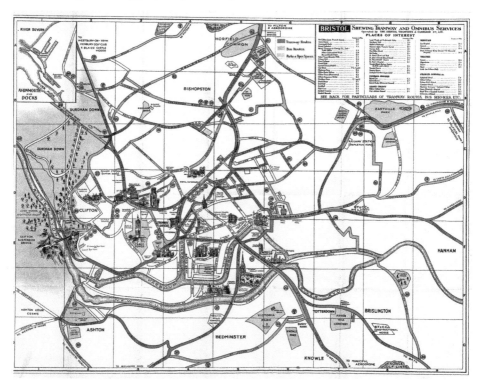

A 1930s map showing tram and bus routes in inner Bristol.

GAE499, C3301, was new in 1939 and had a 56-seat Eastern Coach Works body rather than the home-built Bristol product. It is seen here opposite the Colston Hall and facing the Tramways Centre. (*George Vowles*)

1936-built Bristol JJW CHU567, with Bristol's own 34-seat dual doorway body, sits at the Tramways Centre on Service 18 bound for Clifton during the war, by which time it had become country services' 2042. (*BVBG*)

2002, BHY691, a Bristol JO5G with a Bristol 34-seat dual-doorway body, looks war weary as it stands waiting to take up duty on BJS service 146 between Prince Street and Knowle to the south. The bus has lost its white painted roof, which was never to be re-instated. (*BVBG*)

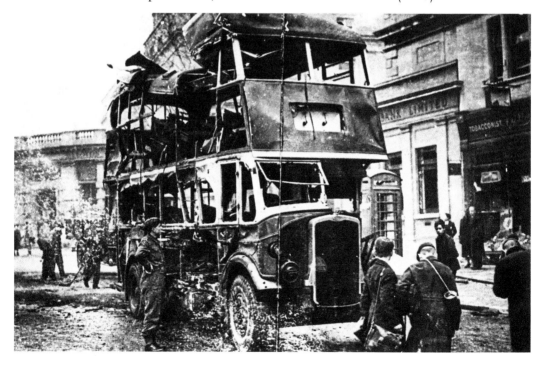

1938 Bristol-bodied Bristol K5G C3161, FHT98, was damaged by enemy action and was fitted with a new Bristol-built body in 1941. (*BVBG*)

Brighton Corporation Transport loaned six 1939 Weymann-bodied AEC Regent O661 models to the Tramway company from 1941 until 1944/1945. FUF77 is shown picking up at the Centre on a country route to Cambridge Batch. These buses principally operated on country services but the occasional use on BJS routes cannot be ruled out. (*BVBG*)

The aftermath of the damage sustained by one bomb falling close to Old Market in the city centre, destroying three double-deckers and causing much loss of life. (*BVBG*)

1933 Bristol B-type HY8880 became C517 and was re-bodied in 1942 with this 1935 Eastern Counties-built body taken from a Tilling Stevens bus acquired from the North Western Road Car Company. Fitted with perimeter seating for 29, it was given a 'V' for Victory prefix to its fleet number. (*BVBG*)

A view of the Bellman hanger supplied by the Air Ministry to replace the just completed Winterstoke Road depot together with the depot staff in the summer of 1942. Two of the borrowed Brighton Corporation AEC Regents are at the left of the picture showing country destinations with two BJS Bristol double-deckers on the right. (*Peter Davey Collection*)

Six London Passenger Transport Board AEC Regents were loaned to Bristol Tramways from January 1944, being allocated fleet numbers 3701–6. One of them is Avonmouth-bound along the Portway, passing underneath Brunel's famous Clifton Suspension Bridge. (*Peter Davey Collection*)

C3000, HY3630, was the very first Bristol G-type, new in 1932 for Greyhound Motors, although it spent six months being demonstrated to other operators before entering service in Bristol. The original body was replaced with the second hand 1936-built Bristol-built body shown here. (*M. Mogridge*)

1931 B-type HY1958 became C438 in 1937, and a driver tuition vehicle in 1947, carrying the number W36 in the works fleet. (*M. Mogridge*)

Bristol JNW-type CHU562 was N97 when new in 1936 with a petrol engine, then C626 and finally C2704 when fitted with a Gardner diesel engine. It was renumbered 2218 and transferred to Bath in 1952. (*Peter Hulin*)

The revolutionary prototype Bristol Lodekka, LHY949, was numbered C5000 (an 'L' prefix was added later). The low build of the Eastern Coach Works body and high driving position are easily seen in this off-side view. (*BVBG*)

During the war years new bus deliveries were allocated by the Ministry of Supply. The only new single-deck buses allocated to BJS were Duple-bodied Bedford OWBs delivered in 1942 and 1943 and they lasted only until 1950. (*BVBG*)

The first of a new design of double-deck bus, the Bristol KS, came to the fleet in 1950, and were the last to be delivered to the old width of 7 ft 6 in. C3477, NAE32, the last of the batch of twenty-two, is shown here at the new post-war development of Knowle West. Note the then comprehensive destination display. Bristol city routes were numbered sequentially with other company routes, so there were often long gaps and very high service numbers! (*M. J. Tozer*)

C3105, EHY567, was new in 1938 as a tram replacement bus. In 1949 it received a new Bristol-built body with a modernised front end, lasting in service for another 8 years. This view shows the 'Festival of Britain' livery adopted briefly in the early 1950s. (*M. Mogridge*)

BJS received only five lowbridge double-deckers, especially for the 36 group of routes. LC3375, JAE763, of 1946, was a K6A with bodywork by Strachan. (*Peter Davey*)

C3409, KHT515, was a 1947 Bristol K6B with Eastern Coach Works 56-seat body. Between 1950 and 1953 it carried an experimental all-green livery. (*M. Mogridge*)

C3296, GAE494, was a 1939 Bristol K5G with 56-seat bodywork by Eastern Coach Works. It lasted in this form until 1954, although the company had to reconstruct the body in 1949. (*BVBG*)

Bristol J 2038, CHU563, from the country services, was modernised and fitted with a new Eastern Coach Works body in 1949. Seen departing the Centre for Clifton, it lasted until 1954. (*M. Mogridge*)

2470, CFH608, was a 1939-built Bristol L-type new to Gloucester City services. On withdrawal in 1954 it became a BJS vehicle so as to respond to a request from the military authorities in Japan for a bus 'from the city of Bristol for the purposes of carrying troops on leave from Korea'. It was shipped east on board HMS *Perseus*. (*Mike Walker Collection*)

C3324, GHT142, a 1941 Bristol-bodied Bristol K5G, was part of a batch used to replace the last of the city's trams, and is shown leaving the central area terminus at Prince Street for Knowle, to the south of the city. (*Peter Davey*)

C2724, JHT859, a 1947 two-doorway Eastern Coach Works-bodied Bristol L5G, served BJS for twelve years. A number of single decks were used so as to provide 'sick man' routes, manned by war veterans who, because of their injuries, may not have been able to easily mount the stairs on double-deckers. (*BVBG*)

New in 1938 as C3135, FAE602 received a modernised front end and a 1950-built 59-seat body in 1955, being renumbered C3483, and in this 1959 view the bus is calling at Westbury-on-Trym en route for Westbury-on-Trym and Stockwood Lane on service 1A. (*Allan Macfarlane*)

Many pre-war buses were re-bodied after the war due to war damage or the previous use of poor materials. C3098, EHY560, a Bristol K5G from 1938, was unusual in receiving a Welsh Metal Industries body and is seen here at Old Market operating eastwards to Kingswood on tram replacement service 8. (*BVBG*)

For a brief period in the early 1950s buses were outshopped in the 'Festival of Britain' livery, with cream around the windows. 1946 Bristol K5G C3396, JHT812, is shown at the Centre about to head northwards to Filton along Filton Avenue. (*Roy Marshall*)

C3082, EAE280, was the prototype Bristol K-type new in 1937 and lasted long enough to be photographed alongside the last BJS Bristol KSW, C8431, in 1957. C3082 was by now twenty years old and on its third body. (*M. J. Tozer*)

The fifty Leyland Titan buses were new in 1947/48 with bodies by Eastern Coach Works, Longwell Green, or, as in the case of C4048, LAE17, seen here in central Bristol while operating cross city service 11, Bristol's own body works. (*BVBG*)

In contrast to C4048 above, C4017, KHW628, had a standard Eastern Coach Works 56-seat body, and is shown here at the Centre heading south to Whitchurch. Some Leylands had black radiator surrounds. (*BVBG*)

70-seat Bristol FLF6B LC8554, 574HHY, entered service in September 1960, cross city service 11 being the first to receive these new buses, the first front-entrance double-deckers in the BJS fleet. In January 1961 it was renumbered LC7004 in a separate number series for Bristol FLFs. (*BVBG*)

C8234, SHW404, was a Bristol KSW6B with ECW 60-seat body dating from 1954. Delivered with a full 36 x 18 inch destination box, it had been converted to an early style of T-box, and is shown here loading at the Centre for a journey to Southmead. (*Geoff Gould*)

New in January 1959, LC8494, 825CHU, is shown here at Lower Maudlin Street, central Bristol, in 1962, operating the long-established 36 route that circled south Bristol. Behind it is LC7001, 571HHY. (*Geoff Gould*)

C3431, LHU978, a 1948 56-seat Bristol K6B, at the service 22 terminus at Sea Mills Square, west Bristol. K-type deliveries ended in 1950 and this bus was withdrawn from service in 1964. (*Mike Walker*)

The successor to the K-type was the longer KS. C3461, NAE16, dating from 1950, is seen at Hengrove, south Bristol, operating cross city route 11 to Oldbury Court. In this view its destination box has been masked down to the new 36 x 12 inch standard. (*BVBG*)

Country service double-deck buses were a not infrequent sight on BJS services as they reached the end of their life, as shown by 1946-built K-type 3671, JHT120. New with a 56-seat Duple body, this was replaced with a 1949-built 59-seat body that had been taken from withdrawn G-type 3036, and in this form it lasted until 1965. (*BVBG*)

C3408, KHT514, an ECW-bodied Bristol K6B, was new in 1947, and, like 3671, had received a newer body in 1957 taken from a withdrawn, re-bodied, G-type. The higher mid mounted gearbox of the G-type necessitated the body sitting higher on the chassis, and when transferred to the K-type this resulted in a higher front end and a straighter windscreen bottom than regular K-types. (*BVBG*)

C8061, NHY983, was a 1952 KSW6B: the KSW was 6 inches wider than the K and KS, and drivers were warned of this fact by the white steering wheel, clearly visible in this view. All BJS KSWs had 4-speed gearboxes and open platform bodies without passenger heaters. The bus is shown operating service 9 over a former tram route to Hanham, to the east of the city. (*BVBG*)

1963 Bristol FLF C7089, 532OHU, is seen here outside Marlborough Street country bus and coach station and depot, where the crew were probably changing over. For a period of time some city services changed crews here in order to make use of the canteen facilities even though the depot operated only country services. (*BVBG*)

Bristol FLF6B C7091, 534OHU, passes under Brunel's Clifton Suspension Bridge having travelled along the Portway and Hotwell Road, the 'fast' road to Avonmouth. (*Geoff Gould*)

Bristol L6B LHY983 was new to BJS in 1949 as 33-seat two-doorway C2743. In 1959 it was transferred to the country services, the rear door removed and used as a one-man bus, and renumbered 2481. In July 1963 it was parked at the entrance to the bus and coach station in Bristol having arrived from Dundry on service 80. This service had earlier been the subject of much discussion at the BJS board as it operated through Bishopsworth in south Bristol before climbing to Dundry, and when, after the war, the city developed Bishopsworth and the surrounding area they felt that this service should come under the BJS umbrella. The company refused and it remained as a pure country service. (*Mike Walker*)

C2764, MHW995, a 1950 35-seat rear-entrance Bristol L5G, started life as country services 2460 but transferred to BJS in 1959 in exchange for a two-doorway model. It is shown at Stapleton in 1965 while operating service 19, one of the few routes remaining in the city at the time that required single-deck vehicles because of low bridges. (*Geoff Gould*)

1949 BJS L-type C2736, LHY976, was transferred to country services in 1960 and renumbered 2495. Unusually, it never lost its rear door and remained two-man operated until its withdrawal from service in 1966. In May 1964 it is parked at Highbridge depot, the most southern outpost of Bristol Omnibus Company. (*Mike Walker*)

As an experiment, two 1964 BJS FLF buses were fitted from new with Leyland O.600 engines, which they retained throughout their working lives. Note the spun aluminium wheel disc, which was an unusual addition to a service bus. C7130, 823SHW, is shown here at Filton. (*Allan Macfarlane*)

The final batch of BJS KSW double-deckers were delivered in 1957. C8415, YHT911, stands at the Bedminster terminus of Service 20 in November 1965 on the eve of a major BJS service revision, and close to the site of the former Bedminster tram depot. (*Mike Walker*)

LC8441, YHT934, a 1957 Bristol LD Lodekka, drops passengers at Lawrence Weston lay-by, west Bristol, in November 1965, operating towards Shirehampton on Service 15, which had been renumbered from 145 a few days earlier in the 1965 service revisions. (*Mike Walker*)

C7207, DHW987C, a 1965 70-seat FLF Lodekka, was delivered with the new scroll fleetname. The bus had painted fibre glass wheel discs on the rear wheels. (*BVBG*)

The 1959 batch of 58-seat LD Lodekkas were the last rear-entrance buses delivered to BJS, and the first BJS buses to be fitted with the Cave-Browne-Cave heating system, identified by the radiators positioned either side of the destination box. LC8535, 992EHW, is seen at St James Barton, central Bristol. (*Photobus*)

1955 KSW6B C8228, SHW398, is shown parked at the west Bristol Cribbs Causeway terminus of cross city service 84. The almost full radiator blind would seem to indicate a cold day. Drivers were advised of 'today's radiator blind position' by means of a mock radiator display in each depot traffic office. (*BVBG*)

The new *City Centre Circle* service was introduced in September 1966 and was operated by Lawrence Hill depot with country services LS (light saloon) and MW buses. Former dual purpose Bristol LS 2927, YHY85, still with dual purpose seats, carries the headboards for the new service as it operates along Anchor Road towards the coach park, September 1966. (*Mike Walker*)

C7108, 801SHW, a 1963 FLF Lodekka, broken down at Lawrence Weston lay-by on 3 September 1966 while operating cross city service 2 to Lockleaze. The conductor, sat on the seat to the right of the bus, is believed to be Robin Orbell, then a conductor at Muller Road depot, who went on to become Managing Director of Eastern National and was later involved in Western Greyhound in Cornwall. (*Mike Walker*)

In late 1966 it was announced that BJS would receive twenty-eight of the new rear-engined Bristol model, the 80-seat VR, and one of the two prototypes, HHW933D, was exhibited at the 1966 Commercial Motor show in Bristol livery. The model never went in to full production and HHW933D was not to come to Bristol for four years. (*Mike Walker*)

Country services KSWs were to be found operating BJS services just before their withdrawal, as had previous types before them. In this July 1967 view 8005, NAE65, new in 1950, is at the bottom of Park Street. (*Mike Walker*)

Country services 388, shown being operated in 1967 by Bristol FSF 6030, 727JHY, ran from Bristol Bus Station to Kingswood, Cadbury Heath and Bitton, all part of greater Bristol, but outside of the BJS agreement. When the agreement was terminated city services were extended to serve all of these destinations. (*Mike Walker*)

A cold December day in 1967 and country services LS 2927, YHY85, of 1957 and 1965 MW 2628, DHW994C, stand at Canons Marsh (old railway goods shed) awaiting departure on the City Centre Circle service. A small number of MW buses received this special, lighter, livery for this service. (*Graham Jones*)

C8110, OHY967, a 1953 KSW6B, leaves the premises of carbon manufacturer Phil Black Ltd at the furthest point of the Severn Road trading estate at the edge of the River Severn to the north-west of the city in March 1968. (*Graham Jones*)

C8124, OHY981, a 1953-built Bristol KSW6G, operates along Henleaze Road, north-west Bristol, in May 1968, on a regular short working schools journey displaying an unusual destination for BJS services, 'SCHOOL BUS'. (*Graham Jones*)

Muller Road depot had a particularly heavy peak operation because of the proximity of the various factories at Filton and Patchway. In July 1968 a line up of KSW buses rests between trips at the front of the depot. (*Graham Jones*)

For a short while before the conversion of services 15 and 83 to one-man operation using 53-seat country services Bristol RELL6Ls, they were used with conductors. 1050, MHW854F, is seen at Lawrence Weston lay-by, west Bristol, on the day before the removal of the conductors, 25 January 1969. (*Mike Walker*)

Country services 45-seat Bristol MW5G 2955, 975DAE, operates BJS service 83 along Tyndalls Park Road in April 1969, on what should be a country services Bristol RE operated route while awaiting delivery of the dual-doorway BJS RE buses. The brackets either side of the destination display indicates that it was also a City Centre Circle reserve bus. (*Mike Walker*)

C8136, PHW961, a 1953 Bristol KSW6B, at Winterbourne, to the north-east of the city and outside of the BJS boundary, on 14 July 1969. It had reached Winterbourne on a schools service and would return to the city on country service 326 – causing yet another mileage imbalance between the company and BJS! (*Mike Walker*)

The very first Bristol FLF LC8540, 995EHW, of 1959, had been renumbered LC7000 in 1961. It is seen in August 1969 loading in Bond Street, central Bristol, while operating lunch time shuttles between the city and the St Anne's industrial area. (*Mike Walker*)

The first of the dual-doorway Bristol REs were new in the brighter 'one-man operated' livery, and put into service in August 1969. C1118, UHU220H, was 'seconded' for six weeks to become a mobile recruiting office, in which role it is seen here at the entrance to Bristol's bus and coach station on 19 August. (*Mike Walker*)

C8224, SHW394, a Bristol KSW6B of 1955, leaves Bristol's country bus and coach station on a duplicate service to Weston-super-Mare on 30 March 1970. It was not unusual to see city buses and crews duplicating country services to the local seaside resorts. (*Graham Jones*)

In early August 1970 the BJS crews held a four-day strike in protest at reduced evening and Sunday running times. The old schedules were resumed pending further negotiations, but as the Old Market (central area) offices and canteen had been closed new arrangements needed to be made for a control room and staff rest room. 1965 BJS FLF C7219, EHT108C, is shown in use in this capacity at Old Market, together with two Morris Minor BRUIN (*Bristol Urban Inspection*) cars used by mobile inspectors in the city at the time. (*Mike Walker*)

BJS dual-doorway Eastern Coach Works-bodied Bristol RELL C1180, YAE443J, was exhibited on the Bristol Commercial Vehicles stand at the Commercial Motor Show held at Earls Court in London in late 1970, fitted with a Leyland O.500 fixed head engine as a test bed for the new Leyland National. Behind the small roof window was the laser generating equipment used by the Marconi bus location system which would identify the whereabouts of the bus by means of a signal reflected from a uniquely marked road side lamp post-mounted plate and transmitted via the bus two way radio. (*BVBG*)

Despite service 17/18 having been converted to one-man operation with two-door Bristol RE saloons earlier in the year, MW C2520, 355MHU, from 1961, operates the service through Clifton in October 1970. (*Mike Walker*)

In tram days the company had a tradition of touring the city with an illuminated tramcar at Christmas, collecting for under-privileged children. The tradition was revised in 1969, and by Christmas 1970 C8318, a 1955 Bristol KSW6B, had been permanently altered to act in this role, having suffered roof damage in an accident with a low railway bridge. In this form the bus was numbered W138 in the works fleet - and boasted a piano on the upper deck! (*Bristol Omnibus*)

Brislington depot closed in August 1971, having been one of the company's first premises, and home to trams, buses and the Body Building Works. A rear-entrance Lodekka can be glimpsed through the imposing archway entrance. (*Mike Walker*)

The depot at Staple Hill, east Bristol, was built to house trams before being taken over by buses, and was closed as a result of the MAP service revision in October 1981. (*Mike Walker*)

C1239, AHU733J, a 1971 44-seat Bristol RELL6L, operates through Fishponds, east of the city, towards the Centre and Clifton. C1239 is fitted with the roof level window used for the Marconi bus location and tracking system, and also displays a comprehensive destination display, something that returned briefly to BJS one-man operated services in the early 1970s. (*Geoff Gould*)

The low bridge at Ashton Drive, south Bristol, was the reason that BJS service 19 remained single-deck and was the first city route to have the conductors removed in late 1968. Unusually, country service 53-seat Bristol RELL6L 1101, RHT150G, is shown passing under the bridge in March 1972. (*Mike Walker*)

C7109, 802SHW, a Bristol FLF6B from 1963, became the first of many overall advert buses in the city in November 1971, and carried this *Berni Inns* advert until August 1973. In April 1972 the bus was seen at the Southmead, north-west Bristol, terminus of service 87. (*Mike Walker*)

Services 22/23 were converted to one-man operation in July 1972, using six of the eight dual-doorway 70-seat Eastern Coach Works-bodied Bristol VRTs that were new in that year, alongside Bristol RE saloons. The drivers for the new service were drawn from the existing two-man rosters, causing some unfamiliarity with the handling characteristics of a double deck bus with a front overhang. On the day after entering service C5009, EHU368K, has come to grief at Sea Mills Square, west Bristol, after possibly impacting a tree. (*Mike Walker*)

Some peak hour journeys on services 77/78 and 87/88 were extended into the back entrance of Filton airfield at Filton West, specifically for factory workers. In this August 1972 view C7288, JAE628D, a 1966 70-seat Bristol FLF6B, emerges from the airfield at the start of its long cross city journey to Hartcliffe. (*Mike Walker*)

The two prototype Bristol VRX 80-seat double-deckers were acquired by BJS in 1970 so as to experiment with single-manned double-deckers. The trade unions would not allow this, as the buses had only one door, and they remained two-man operated during their short life. Unusually, due to their unreliability, both are seen working together here with C5000, GGM431D, ahead of C5001, HHW933D, opposite the old Eastville depot while operating Bristol Rovers football specials on August Bank Holiday in 1972. They were withdrawn the following year. (*Mike Walker*)

Standards of presentation declined during the staff shortages of the 1970s, as exemplified by the blank destination display and 'C' route number suffix on this 1965 Bristol FLF6B, C7201, as it climbs Glyn Vale, Bedminster, heading towards Knowle West away from the city in January 1972. (*Alan Walker*)

Conductor-operated 1964 Bristol FLF C7133, 826SHW, was painted into the brighter OMO livery in May 1971, and one month later the Tilling green areas were repainted into London Country '*Lincoln Green*'. C7133 is seen pulling away from the service 88 stop in the Broadmead shopping centre at dusk two days before Christmas 1972. (*Alan Walker*)

As late as February 1973 the Whitchurch (south Bristol) terminus of the city's most frequent route, service 3, necessitated the bus reversing from the main A37 road in order to turn for the return journey. The driver of 1956 Bristol KSW6B C8363, WHW804, closely examines his near side mirror while performing this reverse. (*Mike Walker*)

Seven months after the conversion of services 22/23 to single-manned double-deckers, reliability still proved to be a problem. Three of the six scheduled Bristol VRTs pull into the Kings Weston Lane stop in Lawrence Weston in March 1973, outbound from the city, although the first and third buses should have been at least twenty minutes apart. (*Mike Walker*)

This Lawrence Hill depot view of 1971 Bristol RELL6L C1217, AHT201J, shows clearly the small city arms emblem displayed above the gold 'Bristol' scroll fleetname carried by buses belonging to the Joint Services fleet. (*Geoff Gould*)

C8370, WHW811, a 1956 Bristol KSW6G, at Lodge Causeway, Fishponds, east Bristol, in May 1973. 91 was a variation of the 89/90 services that connected the Hanham area with north Bristol and the Filton and Patchway aero factories, the 89/90 services being the only BJS route operated by Hanham depot. (*Mike Walker*)

The BJS agreement in a photograph! 1957 Bristol KSW6B C8407, YHT903, crosses the border from Somerset into Bristol in June 1973. From the Whitchurch terminus up to this point the bus was operating 'B', or company, mileage, and the mileage after crossing the boundary was then termed 'A', or attributable to BJS! (*Graham Jones*)

In 1973 the City and County of Bristol celebrated the 600th anniversary of the granting of its Royal Charter with a special event at the Downs. Apart from having a stand at the event, Bristol Omnibus introduced an open top service, 600, linking the city with the display, and used specially converted country service 1956 Bristol Lodekka LD6G L8394, WHY947, which was painted into a special livery depicting various scenes around the city. The bus is seen navigating the Centre in June of that year. (*Alan Walker*)

A Land Rover engineers' van attends to a broken down Bristol VRT at the Lawrence Weston terminus of services 22 and 85 in June 1973. (*Mike Walker*)

In 1973 BJS received a further twenty 70-seat Bristol VRTs, these being delivered in National green livery and fitted with rear route number tracks, although, as one-man operated buses, these were seldom used and eventually painted, or panelled, over. C5015, LHW796L, rests at the Lawrence Weston, west Bristol, terminus of service 22 in July of that year. (*Mike Walker*)

The last BJS Bristol RE buses arrived alongside the double-deckers, also delivered in National green. C1322, MHW282L, passes Muller Road depot in August 1973, just after entering service. (*Geoff Gould*)

Bristol FSF C6015, 714JHY, emerges from under the low St Lukes Road railway bridge, Bedminster, on 19 October 1973 while operating service 98 which connected Knowle, to the south of the city, with Patchway Estate to the north. This particular bridge was the scene of a number of decapitations of double deck buses over the years, and was not the only hazard on the 98 route, as between Knowle and this bridge the bus would have descended the steep Redcatch Road, where a notice affixed to the bus stop at the top of the hill instructed drivers to stop, engage second gear and descend under compression. (*Mike Walker*)

1957 Bristol KSW C8429, YHT925, shown here in March 1974 operating into the city, after cross city service 3 was split in the central area and combined with other services along the Gloucester Road into high frequency trunk routes 73/74 from Patchway and Filton into the Centre. (*Mike Walker*)

LC6016, 715JHY, was new in 1960, and there were only thirteen of these shorter 60-seat FSF model Lodekkas in the BJS fleet. (*Geoff Gould*)

C8379, WHW820, a 1956 KSW6G, leaves Patchway Bus Park for the city in May 1974, but still displays the 'H' suffix used for journeys to the Bus Park. The BJS version of the National Bus Company fleetname has been applied and the bus displays NBC grey wheels. (*Graham Jones*)

Bristol RELL6L C1169, XAE489H, entered service in August 1970 in the green and cream 'one-man' livery, but by May 1975 it had been repainted into National green. (*Geoff Gould*)

1973 saw the delivery of Leyland Nationals and BJS would have no more new single-deck buses built in the city. C1409, JHU850L, picks up passengers on the circuitous 83 route, the first to receive these buses, in February 1976. (*Geoff Gould*)

The 1975 batch of Bristol VRTs were of the VRT/SL3 type with an encapsulated engine compartment and fixed head engines of the Leyland 501 series. C5033, JHW107P, is seen here at Lockleaze (Gainsborough Square), north Bristol, in March 1976. (*Geoff Gould*)

1957-built C8428, YHT924, was one of very few Bristol KSW buses to be painted into full National Bus Company livery, and is shown here in its last year in service, 1976. (*Geoff Gould*)

The 1975 service revision saw the splitting of more cross city services in the central area, the 54/55 being the new services operating from the Centre to Blackhorse and New Cheltenham in the east of the city. 1960 Bristol FSF6B C6010, 709JHY, stands at the New Cheltenham terminus in April 1976. (*Geoff Gould*)

C5032, JHW106P, from the 1975 batch of Leyland 501-engined Bristol VRTs, stands at Filton Church, north Bristol, in April 1977. (*Geoff Gould*)

In common with other National Bus Company subsidiaries, Bristol Omnibus painted a number of buses to celebrate the 1977 Silver Jubilee of Her Majesty the Queen. Country services VRT 5512, LHT722P, a 70-seat single-doorway model, is seen at the centre in February 1978 operating on city services, albeit with a conductor. (*Alan Walker*)

C5083, NFB119R, a 1976 Bristol VRT, speeds through Bedminster East Street in April 1978 on its way to Withywood, south Bristol, passing the premises of W.D. & H.O.Wills, the famous Bristol tobacco and cigarette manufacturer. (*Mike Walker*)

C1219, AHT203J, a 1971 Bristol RELL6L, was delivered in the brighter green and cream livery but, in September 1977, it received an all-over advertisement for the company's pre-purchased multi journey 'Rovercard' tickets. It took part in the 1978 Weston-super-Mare summer carnival, being seen here, on 24 July of that year, working back to Bristol on limited stop service 810. (*Mike Walker*)

In October 1978 the company's penultimate FLF C7312, KHW304E, rests at the Charlton Road, Southmead, terminus of service 88. The last twenty-one buses of this type were delivered without the CBC heating system. (*Graham Jones*)

5113 entered service in February 1978 and by this time the interior trim had changed from green to brown. The bus is shown in November of that year outside the small Avonmouth depot, where presumably the bus or driver are receiving attention, since the service 22 terminus is several miles away and the bus is allocated to Muller Road depot. Avonmouth depot closed in October 1981. (*Geoff Gould*)

At the beginning of August 1979 7294, JHW62E, still displaying the BJS fleetname style, is seen crossing the Centre towards College Green on the frequent cross city service 87/88.

7228, EHT117C, is seen at the Warmley, east Bristol, terminus of service 87. By the time of this August 1979 view the bus had gained the standard fleetname. It was withdrawn in 1983 by then being 18 years old. (*Graham Jones*)

1222, AHT206J, a 1971 Bristol RELL6L, received a colour bus advertisement for HIRERITE and is shown leaving Temple Meads railway station for the central area and Clifton in February 1980. (*Geoff Gould*)

Leyland National 1456, NWS903R, sets off on a journey from Blackhorse, in the east of the city, to the Centre in May 1980. When new the bus was exhibited at the 1976 Commercial Motor Show in a silver livery, was later decorated for HM the Queen's Silver Jubilee and then became an all-over advert for the pre-paid Fare Cards. (*Geoff Gould*)

The route from Henbury, in the west of the city, to Westbury on Trym passed over a ford, although when the local river was in full flood traffic was advised to take the adjacent road bridge. In this November 1980 view the driver of this city-bound service 1 has decided instead to pilot his Bristol VRT through the river! (*Allan Macfarlane*)

The final BJS bus order was delivered in 1980, after its dissolution, and the company was free to allocate these buses as it saw fit. Bristol VRT 5146, AHU523V, was new to Weston-super-Mare to inaugurate one-man operation on the busy town service 105. (*Allan Macfarlane*)

7128, 821SHW, had been new as a country services 70-seat Bristol FLF in 1966, but by the time of this May 1981 view it had migrated to the city's Lawrence Hill depot and was being used on the busy and frequent cross city service 88. (*Geoff Gould*)

Avon County Council supported the 'Windmill Hill Community Bus', which penetrated the steep and narrow streets of Windmill Hill, between Totterdown and Bedminster. Former London Country Bristol LHS, now fleet number 304, RPH105L, descends the narrow streets on a wet day in May, 1981, by which time the service had been numbered 3. (*Geoff Gould*)

At the termination of the BJS agreement outstanding vehicle orders included twenty-three Bristol VRTs and five MCW Metrobus models, as at the time the National Bus Company was keen to trial different types of double-deckers. When they were delivered city drivers were initially given type training, but they refused to use them without conductors and they entered service in Bath, painted into all-over advertisements for the company's range of off-bus tickets. 6000, DAE510W, was borrowed by Weston-super-Mare in August 1981 to take part in the town's summer carnival, and is seen working back to Bath via Bristol. (*Mike Walker*)

5024, MHW291L, from the 1973 batch of two-doorway Bristol VRTs, sets off from the College Green stop to climb Park Street en route for Lawrence Weston to the west of the city. (*Geoff Gould*)

The new double-deck model built in Bristol to replace the VRT was the Leyland Olympian, the company receiving the first of these new buses in 1982, with 76-seat Roe bodywork. A number were delivered in all-over white in readiness for a special livery for Bristol's new network of limited stop services, the City Clipper. However, being single-doors, the city crews refused to accept them for driver-only operation, and they were sent to other depots. 9504, JHU903X, is seen here undergoing driver familiarisation at Weston-super-Mare in July 1982. (*Mike Walker*)

In June 1983, 1966 Bristol FLF 7243, FHT16D, operates from the city towards California Farm on service 87, to the east of the city and outside of what was at one time the BJS boundary. (*Mike Walker*)

In June 1983 7246, FHU59D, a 1966 former BJS Bristol FLF, has climbed Greystoke Avenue, Southmead, bound for Patchway Shadow Factory on service 49 from Lawrence Weston in the west of the city. (*Allan Macfarlane*)

The second batch of Leyland Olympians arrived in 1983, eventually being accepted for single manning in the city. 9540, NTC139Y, is seen here in July of that year, the type having replaced Bristol FLF buses on service 87. All Olympians were fitted with Transign electronic destination displays, with remotely operated rear route numbers, but the equipment became unreliable and was replaced with more normal roller blinds. (*Allan Macfarlane*)

In September 1983 Bristol Omnibus
Company was split into three operating
units and one engineering unit, and
although the company name was retained
for the city and country operations, they
were to operate as separately managed
profit centres under a joint managing
director. The author, being then the manager
of the newly named 'Bristol Country Bus'
operating from Bristol's Marlborough Street
depot, introduced a city Christmas Light
tour in December of that year using 8600,
HOR592E, a former King Alfred Motor
Services and Hants and Dorset Leyland
Atlantean that had been converted to open-
top by Bristol Omnibus for use initially at
Weston-super-Mare. (*Mike Walker*)

Virtually all of the 1980 delivery of BJS-
ordered two-doorway Bristol VRTs stayed
within the city, as exemplified by 5157,
AHW208V, operating Sundays only service
85 to Filton in January 1984. (*Geoff Gould*)

Roe-bodied 1983 Bristol-built Olympian 9544,
NTC143Y, received an all-over advertisement
for the South Western Electricity Board only
months after entering service and is seen here
at College Green in November 1984, leaving
the city for Southmead. (*Alan Walker*)

The last city route to regularly use conductors, the 88, was converted to one-person operation on Monday 23 July 1984 and on the previous day the company organised a Bristol FLF tour. 7262, GAE883D, from 1966 and repainted into Tilling colours earlier in 1984, loads ahead of 7253, FHW158D, outside the company's former head office at the Centre. (*Allan Macfarlane*)

January 1985, and Olympian 9549, A949SAE, heads towards Avonmouth on the 28 route. Delivery of this 1983 batch of Olympian buses ended the company's 75-year association with the Bristol bus factory, which closed during that year. (*Allan Macfarlane*)

Late in 1984 the frequent service between Temple Meads railway station and Clifton was rebranded as CITY B-LINE. Leyland National 1462, NPD110L, new in 1972, came to the company from Hampshire Bus, and is seen here at The Haymarket, central Bristol, in March 1985. (*Allan Macfarlane*)

The final identifiable split between the city and country sectors of Bristol Omnibus came on 29 April 1985, when new identities and liveries were launched to the press at a special event at Bristol airport. Above, a line up of the new liveries for the city, showing the City Rider, City B-Line and City Clipper brands. Below, the new liveries for city and country (renamed Badgerline) show the contrast in the new identities adopted. (*Allan Macfarlane*)

Early in 1984 the city fleet acquired two open-top Alexander-bodied Daimler Fleetline buses from Weston-super-Mare where, in 1980, they had been used to convert the sea front service to one-man operation. In 1985 they were painted to celebrate the 150th anniversary of the Great Western Railway. 5001, LHA615F, is shown in July of that year at the rear of Bristol's bus station. (*Allan Macfarlane*)

In August 1984 the Avonmouth to Withywood services (28/29) received another variant, the 27, as displayed here by 5116, RHT510S, a 1978 two-doorway Bristol VRT shown at Broad Quay, on the Centre. (*Geoff Gould*)

The intended City Clipper branding for limited stop services was introduced in 1985, as shown by Olympian 9515, JHU914X, which had been delivered in overall white. It is shown here at the Haymarket, central Bristol, bound for Lawrence Weston. (*Allan Macfarlane*)

In order to attract publicity to the launch of the first of the high frequency City Dart minibus network in February 1986, the company engaged television personality Leslie Crowther, seen here with a recently delivered Ford Transit. (*Allan Macfarlane*)

In 1982 the company acquired ten two-doorway Bristol VRTs that had been new to Southdown Motor Services in 1972, and which were similar to the company's first eight new in the same year. 5202, WUF529K, is seen here in 1986 at the Lawrence Weston terminus of service 22. (*Mike Walker*)

In April 1986 5076, NFB112R, a 1976 Bristol VRT, passes the Victoria Rooms. From 5075, VRTs of this batch were fitted with power steering from new, with earlier models being retro-fitted following industrial action by the crews that saw them being blacked until so fitted. (*Allan Macfarlane*)

Twenty-five Mercedes-Benz L608D minibuses with 20-seat Reeve Burgess bodywork were new for the first phase of City Dart operations in February 1986. 7491, C491BHY, is seen here in April of that year outside of Dingles department store on Clifton Triangle. (*Allan Macfarlane*)

Seventy-five Ford Transit 190D minibuses formed the backbone of the early City Dart fleet. 7425, C425AHT, fitted with a Carlyle 16-seat body, rests at the Centre, Broad Quay, on its way to the Rookery Farm Estate in south Bristol in June 1986. (*Allan Macfarlane*)

5044, LEU269P, was identical to BJS two-doorway Bristol VR deliveries, but was allocated from new to the company's Cheltenham District Traction subsidiary, which was fully absorbed into the main company in 1980. In 1986 5044 was converted to open-top for the Bristol city tour, and is shown here in July of that year feeding its way through Clifton's narrow streets. (*Allan Macfarlane*)

After the 1985 change of identity, most city bus routes operated under the City Rider brand. 1973 Leyland National 1470, XDL798L, was one of five acquired from the Southern Vectis company in 1985. (*Allan Macfarlane*)

The new City Clipper livery was applied to Olympian 9503, JHU902X, in 1986. (*Allan Macfarlane*)

Forty-five of the 1986 delivery of Ford Transit 190D minibuses were fitted with 16-seat bodies by Dormobile. In June 1986 7472, C472BHY, is operating to Ashton Vale, south Bristol. (*Allan Macfarlane*)

With only eleven days to go to deregulation day and the opening up of the city's bus network to competition, 1980 Bristol VRT 5150, AHW201V, crosses the Downs on its way from Lawrence Weston, into the city and beyond. (*Allan Macfarlane*)

Acknowledgements

I would like to express my sincere thanks to everyone who has assisted in the preparation of this book. A number of people generously supplied material which was of use in compiling the final text and Martin S. Curtis, Peter Davey, Graham Jones, Allan Macfarlane, Barbara Rex and Dave Withers are to be thanked for carefully checking some or all of the text for content and accuracy.

In order to augment my own modest collection of photographs I have been generously supplied with others from which to make my final selection and I hope the result is a pictorial overview of the types of vehicles in use by the company over the years, although limitations on space particularly have influenced this. I am indebted to The Bristol Record Office, Peter Davey, Allen Janes, Graham Jones, Andy King (on behalf of The Bristol Museums Galleries and Archives), Allan Macfarlane and Dave Withers (on behalf of The Bristol Vintage Bus group) for allowing me free access to their photographic archive. In addition, I am grateful to Mike Mogridge and Mike Tozer, and to The Omnibus Society for allowing the use of photographs by the late Roy Marshall. Clive Burlton is to be thanked for supplying the 1930s map.

Photographs are acknowledged individually where the owner of the copyright is known (those from the Bristol Vintage Bus group archive are credited as 'BVBG', while those from the Bristol Museums Galleries and Archives are credited as 'BMG&A'). However, some photographs come from collections which are acknowledged as the copyright owner where this may not necessarily be the case, and I would like to offer my apologies if the reader is affected in this way.

The preparation of this account of Bristol City Buses has been a pleasure and I hope that you, the reader, take as much pleasure from reading this volume as I have in preparing it. Comments concerning the text and photographs are welcome and can be expressed via the website www.bristolcitybuses.co.uk which has been set up specifically for this purpose.

Mike Walker
Wells
Somerset
January 2014

APPENDIX 1: A SNAPSHOT OF BRISTOL CITY FLEET SIZE

YEAR	1923 (a)	1937(b)	1949(c)	1960(c)	1963(c)	1966(c)	1971(d)	1978(e)	1981(f)	1986(g)	1986(h)
S/D buses	62(j)	134	109	14	15	11	101	191	104	79(k)	68(k)
D/D buses	–	55	456	465	477	434	298	149	170	181(l)	161(l)
Minibuses	–	–	–	–	–	–	–	–	–	–	–
Trams	237	232	–	–	–	–	–	–	–	–	170
TOTAL	299	421	565	479	492	445	399	340	274	260	399

NOTES
(a) From *Greyhound Motors, The Story of a Long Distance Coaching Pioneer*
(b) Formation of Bristol Joint Services
(c) Taken from Ian Allan *ABC Bristol* bus fleet books
(d) From *Omnibus*, Bristol Omnibus Staff Magazine
(e) Break up of Bristol Joint Services
(f) At implementation of MAP, October 4th. from *Bristol VR on Home Ground, Volume 2*
(g) At 1 January when Bristol Omnibus Company remained only as the operator of Bristol city buses.
(h) At 26 October, deregulation day
(i) 47 Bristol Tramways, 12 Greyhound, 3 Russett plus spares
(j) Includes two midi buses
(k) Includes two open toppers

Bibliography

Appleby, John B., *Bristol's Trams Remembered, their story 1875–1941*, John B. Appleby, Bristol, 1969

Bristol Joint Services Committee minutes

Bristol Tramways & Carriage Company minutes

Bristol Omnibus Company minutes

Bristol Tramways & Carriage Company/Bristol Omnibus Company/Bristol Joint Services timetables

ABC Bristol, Ian Allan, London, 1949 to 1966

Omnibus, staff magazine of Bristol Tramways/Bristol Omnibus, 1954–1972

The People's Carriage, Bristol Omnibus Company, 1974

Batten, John B., unpublished articles

Bishop, Ian S., *The City & Kingswood Line, A History of Bristol's Trams*, I. S. Bishop, Bristol, 1995

Bruce, Geoff and Walker, Mike, *Greyhound Motors, the Story of a Long Distance Coaching Pioneer*, Bristol Vintage Bus group, Bristol, 2010

Curtis, Martin S., *Bristol – A Century on the Road,* Glasney Press, Falmouth, 1978

Curtis, Martin S., *Bristol Buses in Camera*, Ian Allan, London, 1984.

Curtis, Martin S. & Walker, Mike, *Bristol Omnibus Services, The Green Years*, Millstream Books, Bath, 2007

Dresser, Madge, *Black and White on the Buses*, Bristol Broadsides (Co-op) Limited, Bristol, 1986

Janes, Allen, *Bristol Commercial vehicles, Motor Omnibus operators and Manufacturers, The Early Years*, Allen Janes, Bristol, 2005

Jones, Graham & Macfarlane, Allan, *The Bristol KSW*, Oxford Publishing Company, Oxford, 1985

Macfarlane, Allan, A *Pictorial Tribute to the Bristol Omnibus Company*, 1936–1983, Oxford Publishing Company, Oxford, 1985

Macfarlane, Allan, *The Bristol VR on Home Ground*, volume 1–3, Allan Macfarlane, Bristol, 2010-2013

PSV Circle/Omnibus Society, various publications

From the introduction of the G-type in 1932 until the withdrawal of the last open rear platform KSW and Lodekka buses in 1976, this was the view faced by many Bristol citizens as they ran for their bus. 1956 bus C8374, WHW815, stands at the Henbury terminus of service 1. (*Graham Jones*)